The
Crown
Jewels

Original text by

KENNETH MEARS

Revised with additions by

SIMON THURLEY and CLARE MURPHY

Crown Copyright 1994.

This edition published by the

Historic Royal Palaces Agency 1994.

The Coronation Dates

Coronation dates of the Kings and Queens of Britain since William the Conqueror

WILLIAM I
25 December 1066

WILLIAM II
26 September 1087

HENRY I
5/6 August 1100

STEPHEN
22 December 1135*

HENRY II
19 December 1154

RICHARD I
3 September 1189

JOHN
27 May 1199

Henry III
28 October 1216

EDWARD I
19 August 1274

EDWARD II
25 February 1308

EDWARD III
1 February 1328*

RICHARD II
16 July 1377

HENRY IV
13 October 1399

HENRY V
9 April 1413

HENRY VI
6 November 1429

EDWARD IV
28 June 1461

EDWARD V
Not crowned.
Deposed 25 June 1483

RICHARD III
6 July 1483

HENRY VII
30 October 1485

HENRY VIII
24 June 1509

EDWARD VI
20 February 1547

MARY I
1 October 1553

ELIZABETH I
15 January 1559

JAMES I
25 July 1603

CHARLES I
2 February 1626

CHARLES II
23 April 1661

JAMES II
23 April 1685

WILLIAM III & MARY II
11 April 1689

ANNE
23 April 1702

GEORGE I
20 October 1714

GEORGE II
11 October 1727

GEORGE III
22 September 1761

GEORGE IV
19 July 1821

WILLIAM IV
8 September 1831

VICTORIA
28 June 1838

EDWARD VII
9 August 1902

GEORGE V
22 June 1911

EDWARD VIII
Not crowned.
Abdicated
11 December 1936

GEORGE VI
12 May 1937

ELIZABETH II
2 June 1953

*Date uncertain

The Crown Jewels

ARE the Crown Jewels real and how much are they worth? These are the two most common questions which visitors from all over the world ask the Jewel House Wardens at The Tower of London.

The first question is easy to answer – yes, of course they are real and if you visit the Jewel House on the day of the State Opening of Parliament, you will find the case housing the Imperial State Crown empty because the crown will be in use. As to their value, it is not possible to say. They represent far more than gold and precious stones; they stand for hundreds of years of English history and have been used by English kings and queens since at least 1660. As they stand today, the Crown Jewels are probably the most potent symbols of 800 years or so of English monarchy.

Her Majesty Queen Elizabeth II wearing the Imperial State Crown and holding the Sovereign's Sceptre with Cross and the Sovereign's Orb. Photographed by Cecil Beaton on the day of her coronation, 2nd June 1953.

The Coronation Regalia

The procession of Charles II from the Tower of London to
Westminster Palace on the eve of his coronation, 1661,
by Dirck Stoop (c.1614 – c.1683).

The Crown Jewels displayed in the Jewel House at the
Tower of London are largely those items used at the
coronation of a sovereign and are collectively known as
the Coronation Regalia. Most of the collection dates
from the restoration of the monarchy in 1660, when
Charles II ascended the throne. The old regalia used up
to Charles I's coronation in 1626, had been either
destroyed or disposed of by Cromwell's Parliamentary
Commissioners who regarded it as symbolic of the
"detestable rule of kings". After Charles I's execution
in 1649 Cromwell ordered that the regalia be "totally
broken, and that they melt down all the gold and silver,
and sell the jewels to the best advantage of the

Commonwealth". Luckily, detailed records of the old
regalia survived the Cromwellian era and were used
to draw up a list of new ornaments required for
Charles II's coronation. The new regalia was supplied
by the royal goldsmith Sir Robert Viner for the sum of
£12,184 7s 2d.

Many additions and alterations have been made to
the regalia since Charles II's day. For example, a new
set of regalia had to be made in 1685 for Mary of
Modena, James II's wife, as she was the first queen
consort since the Restoration. Another new set was
required in 1689 for Mary II when she was crowned
with her husband, William III, because she was queen
in her own right and not queen consort.

Up until the early 20th century it was common
practice for some crowns to be set with hired jewels for
the coronation, normally at a cost of 4% of their total
value. For the coronation of George IV, for instance, a
new crown was made and set with hired diamonds

valued at £62,250. Due to the postponement of his coronation, the eventual hire charges for the stones was £24,425. George IV was reluctant to part with his new crown and tried to persuade the Government to buy it outright but it was finally broken up in May 1823. When the hired stones were removed the crown frames were sometimes re-set with imitation stones and placed in the Jewel House for display. The crown of Mary of Modena on show today is one such example. More often, the crowns were dismantled and the frames abandoned. Several of these frames survive and some, on loan to the Jewel House from the Museum of London, are on show today.

The significance and function of the regalia is best understood by reference to its part in the coronation ceremony. The English coronation ceremony, which dates back to the 8th century, has taken place at Westminster Abbey for the last 900 years. It comprises six stages: the recognition, the oath, the anointing, the investiture, the enthronement and the homage. The ceremonies begin with the Sovereign's procession to the Abbey. With two exceptions every monarch from Richard II to Charles II rode in magnificent procession from the Tower of London to Westminster Palace on the eve of his or her coronation. The processions of James I and Charles I were cancelled because of the plague. This Vigil Procession, as it was known, was dispensed with by James II in 1685 on the grounds of economy and replaced with a walking procession from Westminster Hall to Westminster Abbey on the day of the coronation. This tradition lasted over 200 years until the coronation of William IV in 1831. Today the monarch is driven by carriage from Buckingham Palace and is met at the Abbey by those carrying the processional objects.

The portrait of Charles II by John Michael Wright, c.1661, shows the King bearing the new state crown, orb and sceptre made for his coronation. Although the crown no longer exists, the orb and sceptre have been used at every subsequent coronation, including the coronation of Her Majesty Queen Elizabeth II in 1953.

Charles I *by Daniel Mytens, 1631. The old regalia was used for the last time at his coronation in 1626.*

The Processional Objects

···

The Maces

Royal maces began as close protection weapons carried by the king's personal escort – the Sergeants-at-Arms. They later developed into ceremonial staffs carried by the king's officers and today, as symbols of royal authority, they can be used to represent the Sovereign; the House of Commons for example can only do its full business when the royal mace is present.

In the reign of Charles II there were sixteen Sergeants-at-Arms each of whom required a mace. Today there are only three and their duties are purely ceremonial. The maces were traditionally passed from one Sergeant-at-Arms to another and until the 18th century were usually held by the officer who carried them on duty. Thirteen royal maces survive today. Ten are on display in the Jewel House but on State occasions such as the State Opening of Parliament, or a coronation, two are temporarily removed to be

Detail from the coronation procession of James II, 1687, showing one of the King's Sergeants-At-Arms bearing a royal mace.

carried in procession. Of the remaining three, one is kept permanently at the House of Commons, the second at the House of Lords and the third in the Lord Chancellor's Office. All the maces date from the latter half of the 17th century though most have been altered during subsequent repairs.

The Swords

At a coronation three swords are carried unsheathed, points upwards, into the Abbey and continue to be carried throughout the ceremony, but play no active part in the service. They are the Sword of Mercy (the Curtana), the Sword of Spiritual Justice and the Sword of Temporal Justice. It is highly probable that all three swords were made before the Civil War for the coronation of Charles I and survived Cromwell's

The Maces have an average weight of 323oz (10.04kg) and most are some 5ft (152.4cm) in length. The head of each mace is decorated with royal arms and cyphers and national emblems including the rose, thistle, harp and fleur-de-lys.

The Swords of Temporal Justice, Spiritual Justice and Mercy (the Curtana) early 17th century. These three swords represent types that have been used in the coronation ceremony since the Middle Ages. They only became a permanent part of the regalia in the 17th century: for almost 200 years prior to this they had been provided new for each coronation.

destruction of the regalia because they were not intrinsically precious. Evidence suggests that they were used at the coronation of Charles II in 1661 but the first documented record of their use is at the coronation of James II in 1685. They have been used at all subsequent coronations.

The blade of the Curtana has a blunt end which is associated with the legend of Ogier the Dane, who in revenge for the murder of his son, was about to strike down the son of the Emperor Charlemagne when an angel appeared and struck his sword aside, breaking the end of it and saying "Mercy is better than revenge". Consequently, this sword always has a blunt end, symbolising mercy. The sword of Spiritual Justice and the Sword of Mercy both bear the 'running wolf' mark on their blades. This was originally the town mark of Passau in Bavaria but was later widely copied.

Also carried in procession is the two-handed Sword of State, 1678, symbolising the Sovereign's royal authority. It was first used at the coronation of James II in 1685 and has been used by all his successors. It is carried, sheathed, during the first part of the coronation ceremony then exchanged for the Jewelled Sword of Offering when it is required for use. It is also used at the State Opening of Parliament where it is carried before the Sovereign by a senior officer from one of the services.

A second Sword of State, the former Irish Sword of State, is also on display, although no longer used. It was made in c.1660 – c.1661 and was formally held by the Lord Lieutenant of Ireland as the Sovereign's repre-sentative, and on state occasions was carried before him in procession. The sword remained in Ireland until the formation of the Irish Free State in 1922.

The Sword of State, 1678, has a steel blade and a wooden velvet-covered scabbard decorated with silver-gilt motifs including the fleur-de-lys, harp, thistle, Tudor rose, portcullis and the royal arms of William III.

St Edward's Staff, 1661. Made of gold with a steel spike at its end, St Edward's Staff is 56" (142cm) in length and weighs 55oz 19dwt (1.74kg).

St Edward's Staff, 1661

St Edward's Staff was supplied by Sir Robert Viner for Charles II's coronation in 1661. However, its symbolism had long since been forgotten and it has only ever been carried in procession before the Sovereign and laid on the altar in the Abbey where it remains taking no further part in the ceremony. Many legends have surrounded the staff and a Tower of London guidebook of 1831 even claimed that the monde at the top concealed a "fragment of the true cross". Perhaps it can best be likened to the pastoral staff of a bishop.

The Trumpets

There are sixteen silver State Trumpets dating from between 1780 and 1848. Nine are hung with red silk damask banners made for the coronation of Queen Victoria in 1838 but now embroidered with the arms and cyphers of Edward VII and George V (or VI). The remaining seven trumpets are displayed with the banqueting plate.

The State Trumpets have not been used since the middle of the last century when the Corps of civilian State Trumpeters was disbanded by the Duke of Wellington as an economy measure. The trumpets cannot now be played as their present mouth pieces are drilled substitutes: the original mouthpieces were traditionally retained by the trumpeters as their personal property. Nowadays, the Household Cavalry provides trumpeters who use their own trumpets for coronations and other state occasions.

State Trumpets, 1780 – 1848. The trumpet banners are embroidered with gold, silver and silk threads and silk and metal cords. The national emblems of England, Scotland and Ireland (roses, thistles and shamrocks) are embroidered in each corner.

The Anointing Objects

The Ampulla and Coronation Spoon

After the procession into the Abbey the coronation ceremony begins with the Recognition, where the Sovereign is presented to the congregation who signify their acceptance of him or her by their acclamation. Then follows the administration of the oath in which the Sovereign swears to govern his or her people according to the laws of the land, and to defend and preserve the Church. The Sovereign is then seated in the Chair of State and the Archbishop of Canterbury begins the service of Holy Communion. He proceeds as

The ceremony of anointing at the coronation of George VI in 1937. The Ampulla is held by the Dean of Westminster while the Archbishop of Canterbury anoints the King on hands, breast and head.

far as the Creed, when the service is interrupted for the ceremony of anointing. The Sovereign is divested of the crimson robes and leaves the Chair of State to sit in St Edward's Chair (the Coronation Chair) underneath a canopy held by four Knights of the Garter. Holy oil is poured from the Ampulla into the Coronation Spoon and the Archbishop anoints the Sovereign on hands, breast and head.

The gold Ampulla, which is in the form of an eagle, was supplied for the coronation of Charles II in 1661. Evidence suggests that the old ampulla destroyed by Cromwell in 1649 had been small enough to wear as a pendant. The head of the Ampulla screws onto the body and there is a small hole in the beak through which the oil is poured.

The silver-gilt Coronation Spoon is the oldest piece of the regalia. It was most probably made for Henry II or Richard I and is therefore the only piece of royal goldsmiths work to survive from the 12th century. The spoon was sold during the Commonwealth to Clement Kynnersley, a Yeoman of the Removing Wardrobe to Charles I, who returned it to Charles II on the Restoration. Apart from its re-gilding and the addition of four small pearls ordered for the coronation of Charles II, and later replaced for the coronation of William and Mary, it is virtually in its original state.

*The Ampulla, 1661. The gold Ampulla was supplied by
Sir Robert Viner for the coronation of Charles II in 1661.
It is 8.1" (20.7cm) in height and weighs 21.2oz (0.66kg).*

*The Coronation Spoon, 12th century. George IV much
admired the Coronation Spoon and had two copies made
of it set with precious stones.*

The Ornaments

The anointing is followed by the investment with the coronation robes and ornaments, "the outward and visible signs of an inward and spiritual grace". The coronation robes consist of a Supertunica (Dalmatic), an Imperial Mantle (Pallium Regale) a Stole and a Girdle. The Supertunica was made in 1911 for the coronation of George V and is modelled on a Roman Consul's dress uniform. The Imperial Mantle was made for George IV in 1821. Both robes are made of gold thread and together weigh some 23lb (10kg).

From the coronation of Charles II in 1661 up until the coronation of Queen Victoria in 1838, new robes were provided for each coronation. However, since 1911 George V and his successors have all worn the Supertunica and Imperial Mantle currently on display in the Jewel House.

George V wearing the Supertunica and Imperial Mantle at his coronation in 1911. The stole worn by the King was presented to him by the Worshipful Company of Girdlers who also provided a new stole for George VI in 1937. The present stole was made for the coronation in 1953.

The Girdle and Stole were presented to Queen Elizabeth II for her coronation in 1953 by the Worshipful Company of Girdlers. The Stole is decorated with the floral emblems of Ceylon, India, New Zealand, Australia, Canada, Ireland, Wales, Scotland and England. The leek of Wales was used as an emblem instead of the traditional daffodil which would not have shown up well against the gold thread.

The Stole, 1953, is embroidered with the floral emblems of Commonwealth nations; the flags of St Patrick, St Andrew and St George; the insignia of the saints Matthew, Mark, Luke, John and Peter; the Imperial Eagle, St Edward's Crown and the Holy Ghost represented by a dove.

The Spurs, 1660 – 1661

The Spurs, symbolising knighthood and chivalry, are brought from the altar and are applied to the Sovereign's heels, or in the case of queens regnant, simply presented to the Monarch, and returned to the altar. Prior to the Restoration the spurs were actually buckled to the Sovereign's feet. The present spurs were made for the coronation of Charles II but are of a pre-13th century design having a single point at the heel.

The Supertunica, 1911, and Imperial Mantle, 1821.
The Imperial Mantle has a fringe of gold thread and
is embroidered with roses, thistles, shamrocks,
fleur-de-lys and other emblems.

The Jewelled Sword of Offering, 1820, has a gold-covered leather scabbard decorated with the national emblems of England, Scotland and Ireland. The scabbard is set with 1,271 precious stones and the actual sword with 2,205.

The Jewelled Sword of Offering, 1820

The Jewelled Sword of Offering, is then delivered to the Archbishop by the Keeper of the Jewel House and laid on the altar. It is then either girt about the Sovereign or placed into his/her hand before being returned to the altar. It is later redeemed for the sum of 100 shillings and carried unsheathed before the Sovereign for the rest of the service. Until 1902 a new sword of offering was provided for each coronation but since 1911 George IV's sword has always been used. It was made in 1820 at a cost of £5,988 and many pieces of jewellery in the King's collection were broken up and set in it. It has a gold-covered leather scabbard, a blade of Damascus steel and is studded with 3476 precious stones.

The Armills

Then follows the investing with the Armills, the bracelets of sincerity and wisdom. There are two pairs of armills on display in the Jewel House. The gold and enamelled armills of 1661 were made for the coronation of Charles II to replace the jewelled bracelets destroyed in 1649. However, there is little evidence to show that Charles II or any of his successors actually wore them. Queen Elizabeth II was presented with new armills by the Commonwealth nations for her coronation in 1953. They are of 22 carat gold with Tudor rose clasps and were made by the present Crown Jewellers, Garrard & Co. Ltd.

The Spurs, 1660 – 1661. Apart from the addition of new buckles and embroidered velvet straps, ordered for the coronation of George IV in 1821, the spurs have remained largely unaltered since they were made.

The Armills of Queen Elizabeth II, 1953. Beneath the crimson velvet linings the armills are inscribed: "Presented for the Coronation of Her Majesty Queen Elizabeth II by the Governments of the United Kingdom, Canada, Australia, New Zealand, South Africa, Pakistan, Ceylon and Southern Rhodesia."

The Armills and the Sovereign's Ring are clearly seen in this photograph of Her Majesty Queen Elizabeth II, taken on the balcony of Buckingham Palace on the day of her coronation.

The Sovereign's Orb, 1661, (left) and Queen
Mary II's Orb, 1689. In 1671 the Sovereign's
Orb was damaged during a daring attempt to
steal the regalia by Colonel Thomas Blood.

George I from the studio of Sir Godfrey Kneller,
c.1714. The Sovereign's Orb was set with
12 large diamonds, 30 rubies, sapphires and
emeralds for the coronation of George I in 1714.
The stones were valued at £8,200 and hired for
the sum of £328.

The Sovereign's Ring (left) and the Queen Consort's Coronation Ring, 1831. The Sovereign's Ring has been used by all sovereigns from Edward VII to Queen Elizabeth II. The Queen Consort's ring, made for Queen Adelaide, has subsequently been worn by Queen Alexandra, Queen Mary and Queen Elizabeth the Queen Mother.

The Orbs

The Sovereign's Orb is then placed by the Archbishop into the Monarch's right hand before being returned to the altar. It symbolises Christian sovereignty over the earth, the Sovereign being the head of the Anglican Church. The Sovereign's Orb was made for the coronation of Charles II in 1661 and has been used at all subsequent coronations.

William and Mary came to the throne in 1689 each as King and Queen in their own right. Two sets of personal regalia were required for their coronation and a second orb was made for Mary II. It has not been used again at a coronation but both it and the Sovereign's Orb were placed on the coffin of Queen Victoria at her funeral.

Both orbs are hollow spheres of gold. The Sovereign's Orb is 6.5in (16.5cm) in diameter and weighs 42oz 7dwt (1.32kg). Queen Mary's Orb is slightly smaller being 5.75in (14.6cm) in diameter and weighing 34oz 6dwt (1.07kg). Queen Mary's Orb was originally set with hired jewels for the coronation and was later re-set with imitations for display purposes. Charles II's orb, however, was set with precious stones and pearls purchased for his coronation at a cost of £1,150, a figure which also covered the workmanship and cost of the gold. Today the Sovereign's Orb is set with over 600 precious stones and pearls.

The Coronation Rings

The Sovereign's Ring, the "ensign of kingly dignity", is then placed on the fourth finger of the Sovereign's right hand. The present ring was made, together with the Queen Consort's Ring, for the coronation of William IV and Queen Adelaide in 1831. Previously, new rings were made for each coronation and remained the personal property of the Sovereign.

Also on display is a much smaller ring, made for Queen Victoria's coronation in 1838 as William IV's ring could not be adjusted to fit her small fingers. Unfortunately, the jeweller made the ring to fit Queen Victoria's little finger instead of her fourth finger and the Archbishop had to force it on her hand. The confusion was caused by the use of the new finger count. On the old count, the position of the ring would be described as the fourth finger of the right hand, on the new count, as the third finger. Queen Victoria later recorded in her journal, "I had the greatest difficulty to take it off again – which I at last did with great pain".

On her death in 1901 Queen Victoria bequeathed her ring, and those of William and Adelaide, to the Crown and in 1919 they were added to the rest of the regalia in the Jewel House.

The Sovereign's Sceptre with Cross, 1661, is set with 393 gemstones including the First Star of Africa (Cullinan I), the world's largest cut diamond.

The Sceptres

The Sovereign then dons a pair of gloves and receives the Sceptre with Cross in the right hand and the Sceptre with Dove, in the left. Both sceptres were made for the coronation of Charles II in 1661 and have been used at all subsequent coronations.

The Sceptre with Cross symbolises the Sovereign's temporal power under the Cross. It was partly re-made in 1910 to receive the First Star of Africa (Cullinan I), the largest cut diamond in the world. This diamond, which weighs just over 530 carats, was cut from the Cullinan Diamond, found in the Premier Mine in South Africa in 1905 and named after the chairman of the mining company, Thomas Cullinan. The uncut diamond weighed 3,106 carats and a model in the Jewel House shows its original size. It was presented to Edward VII in 1907 on his sixty-sixth birthday by the Transvaal Government and the following year it was cut into nine major and ninety-six minor diamonds. The Second Star of Africa (Cullinan II) is set in the front of the Imperial State Crown.

The Sceptre with Dove, also known as the Rod of Equity and Mercy, symbolises the Sovereign's spiritual role. Like other items in the regalia, this sceptre was often set with stones hired for the coronation.

Also on display are the two sceptres used by queen consorts: the Sceptre with Cross and the Ivory Rod, both made in 1685 for the coronation of Mary of Modena, wife of James II, and subsequently used at the coronations of all queen consorts. They were last used at the coronation of Queen Elizabeth, the Queen Mother, in 1937.

In 1689 the Sceptre with Dove was made for the coronation of Mary II who, as joint sovereign with her husband William III, required her own set of regalia. It has not been used since.

*The Queen Consort's Sceptre with Cross, 1685; the
Sovereign's Sceptre with Dove, 1661; Queen Mary II's
Sceptre with Dove, 1689 and the Queen Consort's
Ivory Rod with Dove, 1685. The first recorded
appearance of the sceptre in the coronation ceremony
dates from the 9th century.*

*George VI by Sir Gerald Kelly, c.1939 – 1945 (detail).
The King holds the Sovereign's Sceptre with Cross,
made for the coronation of Charles II in 1661 and
used at all subsequent coronations.*

St Edward's Crown, 1661

Now comes the actual moment of crowning when the Archbishop of Canterbury takes St Edward's Crown from the altar and slowly, reverently places it upon the Sovereign's head. There then follows a great cry of 'God Save The King/Queen', the princes, princesses, peers and peeresses put on their coronets and caps, the trumpets sound and at the Tower of London a royal salute is fired.

After the coronation of William III in 1689 the role of St Edward's Crown in the ceremony diminished and it was more often carried in procession and set aside on the altar. In its place a coronation or state crown, usually known as the Imperial State Crown, was used to crown the Sovereign. St Edward's Crown was not used at all at Queen Victoria's coronation in 1838 and it was not until George V's coronation in 1911 that it resumed its traditional central role as the coronation crown.

The crown is made of gold and is particularly heavy weighing 71oz 14 dwt (2.04kg). Historically, it was set with stones hired for the coronation and then re-set with pastes so it could be displayed to visitors in the Jewel House. In 1911, for the coronation of George V, the crown was permanently set with 444 semi-precious stones. The crown frame dates from the coronation of Charles II but confusion surrounds its manufacture and it is not impossible that some parts of the crown, or the gold from which it was made, may have come from a pre-Restoration crown.

After the crowning the Sovereign is enthroned (this is the moment when the Sovereign symbolically takes possession of the kingdom) and then receives the homage of the clergy, princes and peers.

The Crown of George, Prince of Wales, 1901 – 1902
This crown was made for Prince George, later
George V, for the coronation of his father Edward VII
in 1902. It was also worn by Edward Prince of Wales
(later Edward VIII) at the coronation of George V in
1911. On his abdication as King Edward VIII in
December 1936 the newly created Duke of Windsor
took the crown to France. It entered the Jewel House
after his death in 1972.

When the Sovereign is a king the service continues
with the coronation of his queen consort who is
anointed, crowned and invested with the queen
consort's ornaments.

*The Crown of George, Prince of Wales,
1901 – 1902, was last worn by Edward VIII,
when Prince of Wales, in 1911. When the
present Prince of Wales was invested at
Caernarvon Castle in 1969 a new crown was
supplied by the Worshipful Company of
Goldsmiths. It is now on loan to the National
Museum of Wales.*

*Edward, Prince of Wales (later Edward VIII)
wearing the Crown of George, Prince of Wales,
at the coronation of his father in 1911.*

Queen Mary of Modena's State Crown and Diadem, 1685

This crown and diadem were supplied for James II's consort, Mary of Modena, to wear at their coronation in 1685. Both were set with hired jewels for the coronation and later replaced with imitations when they were displayed in the Jewel House. Today they are set with crystals and cultured pearls.

The diadem was worn by Mary of Modena in procession to Westminster Abbey where she was crowned with a coronation crown and finally invested with a third, 'Rich Crown' for the closing procession. The latter is the crown currently on display in the Jewel House. Both the diadem and crown were subsequently used up until the 18th century.

Queen Mary of Modena's State Crown and Diadem, 1685, were traditionally set with hired stones for the coronation. In 1685 the diadem was set with 177 diamonds, 1 ruby, 1 sapphire, 1 emerald and 78 large pearls and the crown with 38 very large diamonds, 523 great and small diamonds and 129 large pearls.

Mary II, after William Wissing, c.1690. The State Crown of Mary of Modena rests on the table beside the Queen. Both the State Crown and Diadem of Mary of Modena were worn by her step-daughter, Mary II, at her coronation in 1689.

Queen Mary's Crown, 1911, (left) and the Crown of Queen Elizabeth the Queen Mother, 1937. In 1911 the Koh-i-Noor diamond was set in Queen Mary's Crown for the coronation. In 1937 it was mounted on a new crown for Queen Elizabeth the Queen Mother where it remains today.

The state portrait of Queen Mary by Sir William Llewellyn, 1911 – 1913, shows Queen Mary's Crown as it appeared for the coronation in 1911, set with the Koh-i-Noor diamond.

Queen Mary's Crown, 1911

This Crown, which contains some 2,200 diamonds, was designed for Queen Mary to wear at the coronation in 1911. In the centre of the Maltese Cross at the front is a large, oval crystal interchangeable with the Koh-i-Noor diamond now set in Queen Elizabeth the Queen Mother's Crown. The third and fourth largest stones of the Cullinan Diamond were also set in this crown for the coronation. They were later replaced with crystals and thereafter were reserved for Queen Mary's own use. In 1914 the arches were made detachable so the crown could be worn as a circlet.

The Crown of Queen Elizabeth,

the Queen Mother, 1937

This crown is rather unusual, being the only one in the collection made of platinum. It was made for Queen Elizabeth the Queen Mother for her coronation as queen consort in 1937 and contains some 2,800 diamonds most of which were removed from Queen Victoria's Regal Circlet. The principal diamond, set in the Maltese Cross at the front of the crown, is the Koh-i-Noor (meaning Mountain of Light).

The history of the Koh-i-Noor is uncertain. The earliest legend surrounding it goes back some 3,000 years but it is more commonly thought that the diamond was found in 1655 at the Kollur Mine in the Golconda region of India. It was presented to Shah Jahan by the mine owner and remained in his possession until 1739 when it was captured by Nadir Shah, the Persian King. After a long, chequered history it went from Persia to Afghanistan and thence back to

India. After Britain annexed the Punjab in 1849, the diamond was presented to Queen Victoria in 1850 by the East India Company.

When originally found, the diamond weighed some 787 carats but was disgracefully cut to 280 carats by a Venetian, Hortensio Borgio. Some time later, it must have been cut again as it weighed 186 carats on arrival in England. At that time it was mounted with two other diamonds in the centre of an enamelled armlet, which had been worn by Ranjit Singh, the Lion of the Punjab. This armlet, now set with replica stones, is also on display in the Jewel House. Prince Albert, Queen Victoria's consort, thought the stone badly cut, and after much discussion and consultation, the diamond was re-cut in 1852 bringing it down to its present weight of 105.6 carats.

As the history of the Koh-i-Noor involves much violence and cruelty between men it gained the reputation of bringing bad luck to a male owner. Since its arrival in England it has only ever been worn by queens regnant and consort.

The Imperial State Crown, 1937

The coronation service ends with the Sovereign taking Holy Communion and then withdrawing to St Edward's Chapel to prepare for the closing procession. At this point the Sovereign changes into purple velvet robes, is re-presented with the Orb and the Sceptre with Cross and receives the lighter Imperial State Crown in place of St Edward's Crown. The Imperial State Crown is the best known of all the State Regalia. It is worn by the Sovereign not only on leaving Westminster Abbey after the coronation ceremony but is also worn, or carried before the Sovereign, at the annual State Opening of Parliament.

In 1661, a new state crown was supplied for Charles II, to replace one of the crowns destroyed at the Commonwealth, and was later used by James II and William III at their coronations. For almost 120 years between the reigns of Queen Anne and George IV, the Sovereign traditionally had two state crowns: a temporary state crown, or coronation crown, which was set with hired stones and used in place of St Edward's Crown during the coronation ceremony, after which it was usually dismantled; and a second state crown for parliamentary use which was permanently set with stones. This latter crown was often the refurbished crown of the Sovereign's predecessor, or included stones taken from the previous state crown, and was therefore the repository of many of the stones passing from generation to generation.

The present crown is about the tenth manifestation since the Restoration. It was originally designed and made for Queen Victoria in 1838 and was used at the coronations of Edward VII and George V. It was re-made with practically the same stones for George VI in 1937. For the coronation of Queen Elizabeth II in 1953 the shape of the arches was altered to reduce the height. Although more than 2,800 diamonds are mounted in it, it is perhaps best known for its major stones, famous either for their historical interest or their actual value.

Her Majesty Queen Elizabeth II wearing the Imperial State Crown, and His Royal Highness the Duke of Edinburgh, on the day of the coronation, 1953.

The Imperial State Crown, 1937. Made for the coronation of George VI, the Imperial State Crown is almost a replica of Queen Victoria's State Crown of 1838. It is set with 2,868 diamonds, 17 sapphires, 11 emeralds, 5 rubies and 273 pearls. The crown is 12.4" (31.5cm) in height and, excluding the wire frame, cap of estate and ermine band, weighs 32oz 7dwt (1.06kg).

The back of The Imperial State Crown showing the Stuart Sapphire

In the Maltese Cross at the top of the crown is a sapphire allegedly taken from a ring found on the finger of Edward the Confessor when he was re-interred in Westminster Abbey by Henry II in 1163. Beneath the monde are four large drop-shaped pearls known as 'Queen Elizabeth's Earrings'. Two of these pearls are traditionally believed to have been among the 7 pearls presented to Catherine de Medici by Pope Clement VII on her marriage to Henri II of France, and passed by her to her daughter-in-law, Mary Queen of Scots when she married the Dauphin (Francis II) in 1558. After the execution of Mary Queen of Scots in 1587, the pearls were sold to Queen Elizabeth I. It is suggested that three were later set in Charles II's state crown and were re-set in subsequent state crowns. In 1820 when the old state crown was being renovated one of the pearls was replaced and in 1838, when they were transferred from the previous state crown to Queen Victoria's state crown, a further pearl was added bringing the total to four.

In the cross at the front of the crown is the 'Black Prince's Ruby' which is not actually a ruby but a balas or spinel, a semi-precious stone. It was once worn as a pendant and has small drilled holes in it, one of which is plugged with a small ruby. According to legend, it was owned by the Moors before it came into the hands of Don Pedro the Cruel, King of Castile, who gave it to the Black Prince, son of Edward III, in recognition of his victory at the battle of Najera in 1367. It may have been one of the black balases Henry V wore on his helmet at the Battle of Agincourt in 1415.

Underneath this large spinel is the second largest diamond in the world, the Second Star of Africa (Cullinan II), which weighs some 317 carats. This diamond and the First Star of Africa (Cullinan I), which is set in the head of the Sceptre with Cross, can be clipped together to form a brooch. Queen Mary, consort of George V, occasionally wore them in this manner.

At the back of the crown is the Stuart Sapphire which weighs approximately 104 carats. Its history prior to the Restoration is baffling. The stone was found amongst the papers of the last Stuart, Henry, Cardinal York, in 1807 and was added to the regalia. By tradition the stone had descended from the crown of the Scottish king Alexander II and probably came into the hands of Edward I at the same time as the Stone of Scone. As the story goes, it passed back to Scotland when it was presented to David II by his brother-in-law Edward III and thereafter it remained in the possession of the Stuart family. The sapphire therefore may have followed James II to France in 1688, thereby passing eventually to Henry, Cardinal York. The stone was originally set in the front of the Imperial State Crown until the acquisition of the Second Star of Africa.

The Crown of Frederick, Prince of Wales, rests on a table beside the Prince in this portrait by Jean-Baptiste Vanloo, 1742.

The Crown of Frederick, Prince of Wales, 1728, is of the form prescribed in a warrant issued by Charles II in 1677 which stated that "The Son & Heir apparent of the Crown....shall use & bear his Coronet composed of Crosses and flowers de Liz with one Arch & in the midst a Ball & cross..."

Non-coronation Crowns

The Jewel House also contains three crowns not associated with the coronation ceremony.

The Crown of Frederick, Prince of Wales, 1728

Made for Frederick Louis, Prince of Wales, the son of George II, this crown was used when he took his seat in the House of Lords where it was placed on a cushion in front of him. It was used by subsequent Princes of Wales in the same fashion but was rarely, if ever, worn. It was last used by Edward VII when Prince of Wales.

Queen Victoria by Heinrich von Angeli, 1885. The Small Diamond Crown, seen in this portrait, was worn by the Queen on a great number of occasions including the opening of Parliament. On her death in 1901, the crown was placed on her coffin at Osborne House.

Queen Victoria's Small Diamond Crown, 1870. This tiny crown, measuring only 3.7" (9.9cm) in height and 3.4" (9cm) in diameter, is set with some 1,300 diamonds. After Queen Victoria's death in 1901 the crown became a favourite of Queen Alexandra and was worn by her on many occasions.

Queen Victoria's Small Diamond Crown, 1870

Queen Victoria's Small Diamond Crown was made in 1870 from diamonds taken from a large fringe necklace. It weighs 5.11oz (0.16kg) and was worn on top of the Queen's widow's cap. The Queen was very fond of it and is seen wearing it, both as a crown and as a circlet with the arches removed, in many representations of her after the age of fifty-one. It is said that she disliked the Imperial State Crown because, being a small woman, she found it particularly heavy and the procedures for removing it from the Jewel House too tiresome. This crown has never been used at a coronation ceremony.

The Imperial Crown of India, 1911

Constitutional practice forbids the regalia from being taken out of the country. This ban was probably intended to deter monarchs from selling or pawning the Crown Jewels when they were in need of money. Charles I, for example, had disposed of a large quantity of jewels and plate at the start of the Civil War to raise funds to pay his troops, and it has been suggested that Colonel Blood's attempt to steal the regalia in 1671 was inspired by Charles II who needed the money. Consequently, when George V, as Emperor of India, attended the Delhi Durbar in 1911 to receive the homage of the Indian princes, a new crown was required. It was supplied by the present Crown Jewellers and the cost of £60,000 was met by the India Office. The crown is set with emeralds, rubies, sapphires and some 6,100 diamonds. On George V's return from India the crown was added to the regalia in the Jewel House and has not been used since.

The Imperial Crown of India, 1911, is one of the heaviest crowns in the collection, weighing 34.50oz (0.92kg). After wearing the crown for 3½ hours at the Delhi Durbar, George V later recorded in his diary that its weight had caused him great discomfort.

Detail from G.P. Jacomb-Hood's watercolour (1912) of George V and Queen Mary at the Delhi Durbar in 1911. The King wears the Imperial State Crown of India, made specifically for the occasion.

Altar Plate

....

Gold Chalices and Patens. The gold chalice and paten of c.1661 were supplied for the coronation of Charles II. The second gold chalice and paten and the small gold paten, are of a later date, before 1688, and were most probably made for James, Duke of York, later James II.

Much of the altar plate in the Jewel House is used for the coronation ceremony, either displayed on the altar in Westminster Abbey or beneath the Royal Gallery on the south side of the Sanctuary.

A large quantity of royal plate had been sold off by Charles I in the 1630s and 1640s in order to raise funds and many more pieces were lost during the Commonwealth. When Charles II regained the throne an enormous quantity of plate was required, both for his coronation and own personal use. Between 1660 and 1663 over £30,000 was paid to the royal goldsmith, Sir Robert Viner, for supplying almost two tons of new plate for the King.

Chalices and Patens

All the plate on display is of silver-gilt except five communion vessels (2 chalices and 3 patens) which are gold. The chalice and paten of c.1661 were ordered for the coronation of Charles II. The second gold chalice and paten and the small gold paten date before 1688. All are engraved with the arms of William and Mary.

The Coronation of Queen Victoria *by Sir George Hayter, 1838, showing the High Altar in Westminster Abbey. The large silver-gilt candlesticks and a pair of the 'feathered' flagons are clearly recognizable.*

Altar Dishes

Also on display are a number of large altar dishes including the magnificent dish of 1664 which forms the centrepiece on the High Altar at Westminster Abbey during the coronation ceremony. This dish was made by the London goldsmith Henry Greenaway and is one of the largest surviving altar dishes of the period being some 37.5" (94.6cm) in diameter and weighing 414oz 10dwt (12.89kg). The scene portrayed on the dish is a representation of The Last Supper and the four panels on the border depict The Washing of the Apostles' Feet, The Walk to Emmaus, Christ's Commission to the Apostles and The Coming of the Holy Ghost.

The altar dish and flagon of 1691 were made for the Chapel of St Peter ad Vincula at the Tower of London and are still used in the Chapel each Christmas, Easter and Whitsun. The dish, made by Francis Garthorne and the flagon, by St John Hoyte,

Altar Dish, 1664. *The royal arms depicted at the top right of the dish are those of James, Duke of York, later James II. An almost identical dish made for Charles II in 1660 is in use at the Chapel Royal, St James's Palace.*

were delivered to the Constable of the Tower, Lord Lucas in 1693. Both pieces were used at the coronation of George IV and have been used at all subsequent coronations.

The display also includes a number of flagons made for Charles II including a pair of feathered flagons, dating from 1664 (whose design may have derived from vessels known to have been in Henry VIII's collection); and a pair of large silver-gilt candlesticks, c.1661, decorated with flowers and foliage which were used at the lying-in-state of Edward VII at Buckingham Palace in 1910.

Pair of Altar Candlesticks, c.1661. These large silver-gilt candlesticks measure some 37" in height and together weigh 408oz 7dwt (12.79kg).

Pair of Flagons, 1664. These flagons, together with the pair of 1660, are the largest surviving examples of English flagons. They have an overall height of 20.2" (52cm) and together weigh 420oz (13.06kg). The circular panels on the front of the flagons are engraved with the Stuart arms.

The Maundy Dish, 1660

The Maundy Dish is used by the Sovereign on Maundy Thursday (the Thursday before Easter), for the distribution of monetary gifts to a selected group of elderly people. The ceremony commemorates that part of the Last Supper where Jesus washed the feet of his disciples and commanded them to love one another. A form of the ceremony has been known in England since about the 6th century but from the late 17th century up until 1931, the monarch played no active role in the service and the Maundy was distributed by the Lord High Almoner.

From the reign of Edward III (1327 – 1377) up until the 19th century, the provision of a meal, and the distribution of gifts of food and clothing formed a traditional part of the ceremony. The washing of the

The Maundy Dish, 1660, and pair of Altar Dishes, c.1661. The altar dishes of c.1661 have borders decorated with four oval panels representing on one dish Love, Death, Industry and Strength, and on the other Faith, Hope, Justice and Fortitude.

Altar Dish and Flagon, 1691. This large altar dish, measuring 27.5" (69.8cm) in diameter, is decorated in high relief with a representation of The Supper at Emmaus. Both the dish and the flagon are engraved with the cypher of William and Mary.

feet of the poor was also a central part of the service up until the early 18th century. Today the recipients receive gifts of modern money and specially minted Maundy Money. The Maundy Money consists of one, two, three and four pence pieces in silver, which are the only silver coins still made. Since the reign of Henry VI (1422 – 1461), the number of recipients of the Maundy gifts has been related to the Sovereign's age at the time of the ceremony; the number of coins they receive is also related to the Sovereign's age.

The money is held in white and red leather purses carried on dishes by Yeomen of the Guard. A pair of altar dishes, c.1661, are used to supplement the Maundy Dish. The centre of each dish is decorated with a crowned rose surrounded by freshwater fish, on one dish, and saltwater varieties on the other. As the service takes place at a different cathedral each year the 'freshwater dish' is used at inland cathedrals and the 'saltwater dish' at coastal ones.

The Banqueting Plate

The Plymouth Fountain, mid-17th century. This massive piece, which weighs 454oz 6dwt (14.13kg), is elaborately decorated with flowers and fruit, dolphins, sea monsters and mythological marine figures including four mermaids which support the base.

From the Middle Ages up to the 19th century the coronation ceremony was traditionally followed by a coronation banquet in Westminster Hall. The last such banquet was held in 1821 after the coronation of George IV. It was a particularly lavish affair involving hundreds of guests and huge quantities of food. Some of the ingredients included: 7,442lbs of beef, 7,133lbs of veal, 2,474lbs of mutton, 250lbs of suet, 160 geese, 1610 chickens, 520 hens, 1730 lbs of bacon, 550lbs of lard, 912lbs of butter and 8,400 eggs.

Much of the banqueting plate in the Jewel House was traditionally used at such feasts, either on the king's table or displayed on buffets. The standing salts, of which there are a large number on display, fulfilled an important social as well as practical role: the status of the diner being reflected in where he sat in relation to the salt.

The Plymouth Fountain, mid-17th century
This elaborate piece was presented to Charles II by the City of Plymouth as a symbol of their loyalty at the Restoration. Generally attributed to Peter Oehr I of Hamburg, the fountain was originally silver and was later gilded for the coronation of George II in 1726 and re-gilded in 1821 for the coronation of George IV. The piece has been considerably altered since it was first made but it appears from contemporary accounts that originally perfumed water was fed through the fountain and cascaded into the four large basins. The finial figure was originally that of Hercules, but after the coronation of George III in 1761, it was apparently removed and delivered to a page at Buckingham Palace, and was not returned to the Jewel House. A new figure, possibly representing Cleopatra and the Asp, was made for the coronation of George IV.

The Exeter Salt, c.1630, is set with over 70 gemstones including emeralds, rubies, amethysts, sapphires and turquoises. These stones were cleaned and re-set, or replaced, before each coronation.

The Exeter Salt, c.1630

The Exeter Salt, or Salt of State, was another gift presented to Charles II at the Restoration, this time by the City of Exeter. It bears the mark of the German goldsmith Johann Hass. Many theories have been expounded about its design: the upper half has been likened to the old Pharos (lighthouse) of Alexandria, the seventh wonder of the world, and the lower half has been said to be a model of the White Tower at the Tower of London. All the turrets can be removed and underneath each is a small receptacle which holds about an ounce of salt. Other concealed drawers would have been used for pepper and spices.

St. Georges' Salts, 1660 – 1661

The probable origin of the eleven St. Georges' salts was a banquet organised by the Knights of the Garter and held in the presence of Charles II on 15th April 1661, in honour of St George's Day. There were originally 6 sets each of four salts: one set for the King's table, 4 sets for the Knights' tables, and a further set for the Officers of the Order. The King's set are shaped like hourglasses while those for the Knights have circular bodies. All are surmounted with canopies bearing an armed equestrian figure. The salts for the Officers of the Order have napkin brackets around the salt wells instead of canopies.

*The Queen Elizabeth Salt, 1572 (left), and two
St George's Salts, c.1661. The Queen Elizabeth
Salt was placed with the St George's Salts in the
late 17th century to replace one which had
become lost or damaged.*

In 1680 a large quantity of Jewel House plate was
melted down to provide funds for Charles II and it is
thought that twelve of these salts were destroyed at this
time, leaving the King's set, the Officer's set and one
each of the four Knight's sets. A further salt was lost
around the time of William and Mary's coronation in
1689 and was replaced with the Queen Elizabeth Salt.

When the four salts of the Officers of the Order
were being prepared for the coronation banquet of
George IV in 1821, the crown jewellers mistook the
brackets for legs, turned the salts upside down and
fitted new salt dishes into their bases. The salts were
thus displayed upside down for nearly a hundred years
until 1906 when William Watts, Keeper of Metalwork
at the Victoria & Albert Museum, noticed the error.

There are also twelve salt spoons on display which
were made in 1820 for the coronation of George IV
and are engraved with his royal arms.

The Queen Elizabeth Salt, 1572

The Queen Elizabeth Salt of 1572 has been attributed
to the London goldsmith Affabel Partridge known to

have been working for the Queen from about 1558 – 1576. The salt, however, is not identifiable in any royal inventory before the second half of the 17th century and is therefore unlikely to have actually belonged to Queen Elizabeth I. It is suggested that the salt was most probably acquired for the Crown at the time of the Restoration and the presence of Charles II's cypher beneath one of the feet helps support this theory.

The main body of the salt is decorated with three panels depicting, in relief, the figures of the virtues Faith, Hope and Fortitude. The three circular panels on the domed cover contain the figures of Ceres, Lucretia and Cleopatra.

The armed figure surmounting the cover bears a large sword in his left hand. The prop in his right is thought to be the original support of an emblem or coat of arms long since lost. Inside the cover is engraved the Tudor rose.

The main body and cover are separated by a detachable frame with scroll brackets supported by dolphins. This frame was added to the salt in the early 17th century to allow easier access to the salt bowl.

The Caddinets

Unlike the majority of the banqueting plate in the Jewel House which was reserved for use at coronation banquets, the two caddinets on display were most likely used as everyday pieces by royalty. They functioned as place settings with the small lidded box on the left of the tray containing the salt and the longer one on the right, the cutlery.

The caddinet of 1683 was made for Charles II and originally bore his coat of arms; it is now engraved with the arms of William and Mary. The second, caddinet of 1688, also bears the arms of William and Mary but of the period prior to their recognition by Scotland. Hence, both the second and third quarters of the shield are occupied by the Irish Harp while the second supporter is not the Scottish Unicorn but the Tudor Dragon.

George Jones, The Banquet at the Coronation of George IV, 1821 *(detail). This painting records the last coronation banquet to be held in Westminster Hall. Today the Sovereign traditionally dines at Buckingham Palace after the coronation.*

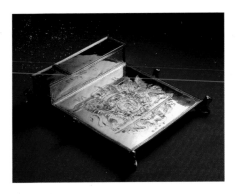

Caddinet, 1688. The caddinet was introduced to England by Charles II who had admired their use at the French Court. The caddinets on display in the Jewel House are two of the very few surviving English pieces of the form.

*The Wine Cistern, or Grand Punch Bowl, 1829, weighs
8000oz (257.23kg) and measures 30" (76.2cm) in height,
54.5" (138.5cm) in length and 40" (101.5cm) in width.*

*The Ladle for the Grand Punch Bowl, 1841. Made of ivory
and silver-gilt, the ladle was supplied by the goldsmiths
E.E.J. & W. Barnard for the christening of Queen Victoria's
eldest son, Albert Edward, Prince of Wales.*

The two caddinets were probably sold in 1808 with other surplus plate to defray the expenses of the Princess of Wales, Caroline of Brunswick, wife of George IV. They were subsequently in the collection of the Earl of Lonsdale and in 1975 were jointly acquired by H.M. The Queen and the British Government from Lord Lonsdale's estate.

The Wine Cistern, 1829

The Wine Cistern, or Grand Punch Bowl, was supplied for George IV in 1829 by the Crown Jewellers of the day, Rundell, Bridge and Rundell. It bears the maker's mark of John Bridge. It is said to be the heaviest recorded surviving piece of English plate weighing some 8,000oz, or nearly a quarter of a ton (257.23kg). The upper section of the body is elaborately decorated with Bacchanalian scenes and the lower half is encrusted with rocks, shells and all manner of marine life. The interior is engraved with the royal arms of George IV.

The Wine Cistern can hold 144 bottles of claret which would have been cooled with ice and damp cloths as claret was often not served at room temperature in the 19th century.

In 1842 the Wine Cistern was used as a punch bowl for the christening of Albert Edward, Prince of Wales, Queen Victoria's eldest son and later Edward VII. For this purpose a ladle was made in 1841, the bowl of which represents a large conch shell. The handle is engraved with the arms of the Prince of Wales and an inscription recording its use at the christening.

Tankards, mid-17th century

The display also includes two covered tankards supplied for the coronation of Charles II. They are elaborately decorated with Bacchanalian scenes in high relief and bear the mark of the goldsmith Hans Lambrecht III of Hamburg. In the 18th century they were used at a number of royal christenings with the Charles II Font.

Detail of Banquet in the Picture Gallery, Buckingham Palace, 1853 *by Louis Haghe. Note the magnificent display of plate on the buffet at the far end of the room. The banqueting plate on show in the Jewel House would have been displayed in a similar manner at the traditional coronation banquet in Westminster Hall.*

The Christening Fonts

The Charles II Font and Basin, 1660. The font and basin
are both finely chased with flowers and foliage and the
arms and cypher of Charles II. The bowl of the font is
decorated with six cherubs holding emblems of
martyrdom and the final group on the domed cover is
that of St Philip baptizing the Eunuch.

*The Christening Ewer and Basin, c.1735, are both
engraved with the royal arms of George III. The handle of
the ewer is surmounted by the figure of Hercules slaying
the Hydra.*

The Charles II Font and Basin, 1660

Although Charles II was unmarried when he came to
the throne he persuaded the Treasury to pay for a
magnificent christening font and basin. His subsequent
marriage to Catherine of Braganza produced no
children but it is thought that the font was used to
christen some of his illegitimate children, of which he
had at least thirteen. The font was used for royal
christenings up to the late 18th century and its last
recorded use appears to be for the christening of
Princess Charlotte in 1796. The basin was used as an
altar dish at the coronations of George IV and Queen
Victoria and is now on display with the altar plate.

Christening Ewer and Basin, c.1735

The Ewer and Basin were first used for the christening
of the future King George III at Norfolk House in
1738. His father, Frederick, Prince of Wales, had been
banished from the court of George II and was denied
the use of the Charles II Font. Both pieces are engraved
with the royal arms of George III and an inscription
recording their use at his christening and the subsequent
christening of his son, Prince Alfred, in 1780.

The Lily Font, 1840

This silver-gilt christening font was made by E.E.J. &
W. Barnard for the baptism of the Princess Royal,
Queen Victoria's first child, in 1841. It was said that
Queen Victoria did not care for the Charles II
Christening Font because of its links with his
illegitimate children. The base of the font bears the
coats of arms of the Princess Royal, Prince Albert and
the joint arms of Queen Victoria and Prince Albert.

The Lily Font is still used by the Royal Family
today and with it, the 1735 Ewer.

The Lily Font, 1840, is still used by the Royal Family today together with the christening robe made for the Princess Royal in 1841.

The Lily Font is clearly depicted in this painting by Charles Robert Leslie which records the christening of the Princess Royal in the Throne Room of Buckingham Palace, 10 February 1841 (detail).

The History of the Display of the Crown Jewels

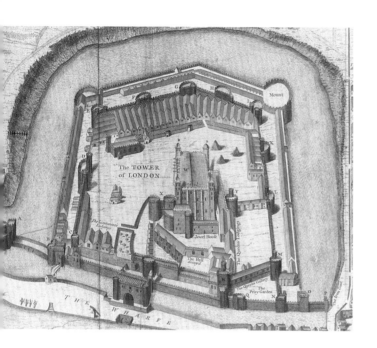

Before the Restoration the regalia was kept in a building erected by Henry VIII in the 1530s on the south side of the White Tower.

The history of the display of the Crown Jewels to the public only really begins after the Restoration of Charles II in 1660. Before then, the old regalia was stored, together with the royal plate, in a building adjacent to the White Tower, erected by Henry VIII in the 1530s. Immediately after the coronation of Charles II in 1661, the new regalia, made for the occasion, was placed there but this was only a temporary solution for in 1669, the lower chamber of the Martin Tower, situated in the north-east corner of the inner ward, was designated as their new home. The jewels were to be placed in the lower chamber and the Keeper of the

Jewels was moved from his residence near the old Jewel House in Coldharbour to the upper Martin Tower in June 1669.

The apartments on the first floor of the tower were not in fact occupied by Sir Gilbert Talbot, the Master of the Jewel House, who had no wish to live there but by a deputy called Talbot Edwards. Edwards had no salary as Talbot could not afford to pay him one, and so he was licensed to show the regalia to visitors in return for a small fee. This was done very informally to begin with, Edwards taking the regalia out of a locked cupboard to show it. But in 1671 the inevitable occurred – someone took advantage of the lax and informal arrangements and attempted to steal the Crown Jewels.

Colonel Blood

Colonel Thomas Blood's attempt to steal the Crown Jewels was very professionally planned and, was, in the end, only foiled by bad luck. In April 1671, he visited Talbot Edwards to view the jewels disguised as a clergyman, with a female accomplice, supposedly his wife. Further visits ensued and as Mr and Mrs Edwards became friends with their pious visitors, it emerged that a match might be made between Edwards's daughter and a nephew of Blood's. A date was therefore arranged for the young couple to meet.

The Jewel House in the lower Martin Tower, c.1820. Notice the State Crown and Exeter Salt. They are displayed under glass bells on clockwork turntables.

On the 9th May, Blood arrived for his appointment with three accomplices, one of whom was his alleged nephew and the prospective suitor. While they waited for Mrs Edwards and her daughter to come down, Blood suggested that they view the Crown Jewels. On opening the Jewel House for his visitors, Edwards was coshed, bound and gagged. Blood, acting quickly, seized the crown and put it under his cape, one accomplice thrust the orb into his breeches while the third grabbed the sceptre. To this point, the raid had gone like clockwork but suddenly their luck ran out as Edwards's son unexpectedly appeared on leave from his regiment in Flanders. His arrival caused the robbers to flee, dropping the sceptre and making for waiting horses on the Wharf. There, they were apprehended and taken into custody.

All this ended the informal arrangements for viewing the regalia set up after the Restoration. An armed guard was now provided and when visitors were admitted again there was a broadsheet listing the jewels on show. It was, in effect, the first edition of this guidebook and almost all the items listed in it are still on display today.

Visiting the Jewels in the 18th Century

Visiting the jewels in the early 18th century with broadsheet in hand was a very different experience to that which visitors have today. Visitors were locked into the lower Martin Tower, an armed guard was posted outside and they were seated on benches from which the regalia could be viewed. For a small additional fee, visitors could reach through the bars, feel the weight of the jewels and even try on the armills. The room was windowless and candles and lanterns flickered in the gloom.

The keepers were wholly responsible for the display of the regalia and this inevitably led to problems. The Keeper of the Jewels between 1702 and 1719 was Talbot Edwards Junior. He became increasingly worried about their security and decided to replace, at his own expense, the rather flimsy wooden bars protecting the jewels with iron ones. On his death in 1719, his executors announced that the bars were theirs and that they were going to remove them. The Office of Works had to pay £14 8s 4d to buy the bars and secure the safety of the jewels.

Another incident in 1815 led to more changes being made to the displays. That year, a woman visitor (later found by a magistrate to be insane) got hold of the State Crown and wrenched its arches apart causing over £10 worth of damage. This, and the poor quality of the Keeper's accommodation led to a major modernisation of the Jewel House. In 1816, the jewels were removed and over £730 was spent on

*A broadsheet listing the regalia on display to the
public in the early 18th century.*

*The Martin Tower as the Jewel House
in the early 19th century.*

modernising the display and the residence above. A rail
was introduced to keep the public away from the
regalia, turntables were installed and on them, under
glass cases, were placed the State Crown and the Exeter
Salt. Eventually oil lamps, for better viewing, were
provided. But conditions were still not ideal and there
were complaints that the new bars were so close
together that no-one could see the jewels.

Plans for a new Jewel House

Improvements to the display and the general popularity
of the regalia made the office of the Keeper of the Jewel
House a very lucrative one. In the early 1830s, he was
earning up to £550 a year, a considerable sum. After
1838 when the entrance fee to the Tower as a whole
was reduced, there was a surge of visitors and the
Keeper's income soared to £1500 a year. The Treasury,
hardly surprisingly, was unwilling for this situation to
continue. It bore the liabilities for the display and
received none of the benefits. So in 1840, new
arrangements were planned. A new jewel house would
be built which would provide better viewing facilities
and admit more people. An entrance charge of 6d
would be levied and the Keeper put on a fixed salary.
Unfortunately, these plans were held up by the next
great event in the history of the Crown Jewels – the
Fire of 1841.

The Fire of 1841

On the night of 30 – 31st October 1841, the Great
Storehouse directly adjacent to the Jewel Tower went
up in flames. It was impossible to know where the fire
would stop and there were fears for the safety of the
jewels. Before long the decision was taken to evacuate
them. Unfortunately in the interests of security, the keys
were in the possession of the Lord Chamberlain whose
whereabouts was unknown and so it was decided to
force the bars of the case apart with a crowbar to
remove the jewels. The superintendent of police himself
pulled the jewels out of the partially demolished
display case and only with extreme difficulty managed
to extract the Plymouth Fountain which was too large
to fit through the forced opening.

The 1842 Jewel House

After the fire, the jewels were not returned to public
display until March 1842 when they were installed in
a new Jewel House next to the Martin Tower. This
incorporated several innovations for visitors. The
jewels were now in a glass cage in the middle of the
room which allowed visitors to circulate round them.
This was surrounded by a low stone wall topped with a
railing. The room was lit by large windows.

All this sounds like a great improvement, much
better than the displays which were formally in the tiny
medieval basement of the Martin Tower. But there were
severe problems with the new display – reflection on
the glass made the jewels impossible to see; the light
was in the wrong place; the building was damp and
both fire and security inspectors condemned it as
seriously inadequate. Only 12 years after its
completion, the Duke of Wellington said that the new
Jewel House ought to be demolished. This was easier
said than done because a suitable space had to be
found for an alternative display elsewhere in the Tower
of London.

The day after the 1841 fire, George Cruikshank drew
this scene of the rescue of the Crown Jewels based
on first-hand accounts.

The new Jewel House of 1842. Immediately to its left
is the Martin Tower, the old home of the jewels and
the residence of the Jewel Keeper.

The interior of the Jewel House of 1842. At first sight, a great improvement but in reality it had to be replaced within 30 years of opening.

The Jewel House of 1868 in the upper Wakefield Tower. The interior was re-modelled by Anthony Salvin and the display was arranged by the Crown Jewellers, Garrard & Co. Ltd.

The display in the upper Wakefield Tower in 1967.

The display in the upper Wakefield Tower immediately before the Crown Jewels were moved to the new Jewel House in 1967.

The 1868 Jewel House

Eventually a proposal was made which allowed space to be found on the first floor of the Wakefield Tower and a residence for the Keeper to be formed in St Thomas's Tower next door. The cost of the works, to be undertaken by the architect Anthony Salvin, was £3,181. Work started in August 1867 removing much of the medieval interior of the Wakefield Tower, inserting a new stone vault and building a bridge to link it with St Thomas's Tower. A new display case was designed by Salvin, surrounded by a magnificent Gothic grill. Inside it, the Crown Jewellers, Garrard & Co. Ltd, designed a new setting for the jewels at a cost of £510. The new building received the jewels in April 1868. The Wakefield Tower remained the home of the Crown Jewels for almost exactly 100 years, during which time the display case itself was refurbished twice, in the interests of greater security and better presentation.

After the Second World War, there was talk of moving the jewels from the Wakefield Tower to a more spacious and secure location. A scheme was devised to celebrate the coronation of Queen Elizabeth II whereby the jewels would be moved to the Waterloo Barracks. This was abandoned, but during the 1950s suggestions were made for an underground bomb-proof Jewel House, one near the Lanthorn Tower and another under Chapel Green. For various reasons, neither of these came to fruition. By 1960 visitor pressure on the Jewel House was enormous – on peak days there were over 1,250 visitors, and so the decision was taken to build a new underground Jewel House near the Waterloo Barracks. This was completed in 1967 and the jewels were installed there in a star-shaped case by the designer Alan Irvine.

The underground Jewel House was home to the jewels right through the Cold War, through the 1980s and into the early 1990s. During this time the display was refurbished twice, most recently in 1988. By then, up to 15,000 people a day were descending the 49 steps to see the jewels causing queues up to an hour long. These queues were the principal factor which led to a decision in 1992 to bring the jewels up to the surface again and put them in a much enlarged space on the ground floor of the Waterloo Barracks. The new Jewel House was opened by Her Majesty The Queen on 24th March 1994.

The display in the Jewel House of 1967 as first installed by Alan Irvine.

ACKNOWLEDGEMENTS

Photography by
DAVID CHALMERS

Designed by
ALTER EGO

Printed in England by
ROYLE PRINT LIMITED

Typesetting by
SHARP IMAGE

Project Co-ordinator
MARK McVAY

With special thanks to
David Thomas the Crown Jeweller, and the
Curators and Wardens of the Jewel House for their assistance
during the photography of the Crown Jewels.

The Curators and Wardens of the Jewel House